When I Survey

a 12-day hymnological journey to the cross

Copyright Kim Sorgius 2016.

ALL RIGHTS RESERVED. This book contains material protected under International and Federal Copyright Laws and Treaties. Any unauthorized reprint or use of this material is prohibited. No part of this book may be reproduced or transmitted in any form or by any means, electronic or mechanical, including photocopying, recording, or by any information storage and retrieval system without express written permission from the author / publisher.

Unless otherwise indicated, all Scripture quotations are from The Holy Bible, English Standard Version® (ESV®), copyright © 2001 by Crossway, a publishing ministry of Good News Publishers. Used by permission. All rights reserved.

All Scripture quotations marked (KJV) are from The Holy Bible, King James Version. Public Domain.

The purchaser of this ebook has permission to print unlimited copies of the ebook text and journal for immediate family use only. For any group consisting of more than one immediate family, each family is required to purchase a copy of this ebook.

TABLE OF CONTENTS

Hosanna Loud Hosanna

Are you Washed in the Blood?

At the Cross

Crown Him With Many Crowns

Grace Greater Than Our Sin

There is a Fountain

Jesus Paid it All

Christ Arose

Christ the Lord is Risen Today

He Lives

HOW TO USE THIS STUDY

I have written this unit study with the busy family in mind. There are many ways to adapt it to fit your needs. As written, the study spans 12 days. Of course, you can go slower or faster, should you desire. A simple family devotion that includes the Bible reading and singing of the hymn could be done in 15 minutes!! Of course, the full study could be used in place of a regular school day. It's completely up to you.

Each day you will journey to the cross through the following activities:
~Bible reading
~Hymn
~Suggested act of service
~Notebooking page for the hymn
~Activity page
~Copywork

Of course, it's up to you how much of the study you complete. Short on time? Skip the notebooking page. Want to keep it simple? Leave out the activity page. I hope you will find the study incredibly flexible to meet your needs. Copywork is included for each hymn, both in KJV and ESV. These are located in the appendix for easier printing. Simply choose the translation that you prefer and then slip them into the right sections. Each page is labeled with the corresponding day at the bottom.

If you plan to have your child take notes on the hymn, you will want to print 12 copies of the hymn notebooking page. You will find it directly after this page.

Please don't hesitate to email me with questions or feedback at kim@notconsumed.com!

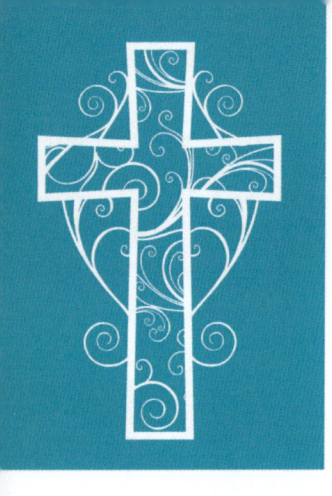

Hosanna Loud Hosanna

DAY 1

1 Hosanna, loud hosanna,
the little children sang,
through pillared court and temple
the lovely anthem rang.
To Jesus, who had blessed them
close folded to his breast,
the children sang their praises,
the simplest and the best.

2 From Olivet they followed
mid an exultant crowd,
the victor palm branch waving,
and chanting clear and loud.
The Lord of earth and heaven
rode on in lowly state,
nor scorned that little children
should on his bidding wait.

3 "Hosanna in the highest!"
that ancient song we sing,
for Christ is our Redeemer,
the Lord of heaven our King.
O may we ever praise him
with heart and life and voice,
and in his blissful presence
eternally rejoice!

©Not Consumed 2016 | When I Survey

HYMN STUDY Notes

Name of the hymn _____

This hymn was written by _____

This hymn was written in _____

This hymn writer wrote _____ hymns.

Some facts about the author:

_____

_____

_____

_____

Tell a little about the story behind the hymn.

_____

_____

_____

_____

DAY 1   ©Not Consumed 2016 | When I Survey

Hosanna LOUD HOSANNA

TIME IN THE WORD:

Read Matthew 21:1-11. Write 3 interesting facts from the passage.

_____

_____

_____

What did the people shout as they saw Jesus?

_____

Look up the word Hosanna in a Bible dictionary. What does it mean?

_____

TIME IN SONG:

Sing Hosanna, Loud Hosanna (http://bit.ly/2dmcHTq). Read the story behind it and fill out your notebook page.

TIME IN SERVICE:

Clear branches or debris from your yard or a neighbor's yard.

Make an arrival basket for out of town Easter guests.

Hosanna, Loud Hosanna

1 Hosanna, loud hosanna the little children sang;
through pillared court and temple the lovely anthem rang.
To Jesus, who had blessed them, close folded to his breast,
the children sang their praises, the simplest and the best.

2 From Olivet they followed mid an exultant crowd,
the victory palm branch waving, and chanting clear and loud.
The Lord of earth and heaven rode on in lowly state,
nor scorned that little children should on his bidding wait.

3 "Hosanna in the highest!" That ancient song we sing,
for Christ is our Redeemer, the Lord of heaven, our King.
O may we ever praise him with heart and life and voice,
and in his blissful presence eternally rejoice.

Text: Jennette Threlfall, 1873
Tune: *Gesangbuch*, Wittenberg, 1784

76 76 D
ELLACOMBE

www.hymnary.org/text/hosanna_loud_hosanna_the_little_children

This hymn is in the public domain. You may freely use this score for personal and congregational worship. If you reproduce the score, please credit Hymnary.org as the source.

Crossword Puzzle   HOSANNA

Use Matthew 21:1-11 to complete the crossword puzzle.

hosanna   cloaks   king   colt   jesus   shout   donkey   branches

Across
2. They found a _____ and its colt
3. The animal that Jesus rode.
6. A word that means "save us."
7. Something said in a loud voice

Down
1. They waved _____ from the trees.
3. They spread their _____ on the ground.
4. The Scriptures said, "Behold your _____ will come riding on a donkey."
7. the Son of God

©Not Consumed 2016 | When I Survey

Are You Washed in the Blood?

DAY 2

1 Have you been to Jesus for the cleansing power?
Are you washed in the blood of the Lamb?
Are you fully trusting in His grace this hour?
Are you washed in the blood of the Lamb?

Refrain
Are you washed in the blood,
In the soul cleansing blood of the Lamb?
Are your garments spotless? Are they white as snow?
Are you washed in the blood of the Lamb?

2 Are you walking daily by the Savior's side?
Are you washed in the blood of the Lamb?
Do you rest each moment in the Crucified?
Are you washed in the blood of the Lamb?

3 When the Bridegroom cometh will your robes be white?
Are you washed in the blood of the Lamb?
Will your soul be ready for the mansions bright,
And be washed in the blood of the Lamb?

4 Lay aside the garments that are stained with sin,
And be washed in the blood of the Lamb;
There's a fountain flowing for the soul unclean,
O be washed in the blood of the Lamb!

©Not Consumed 2016 | When I Survey

Are You Washed IN THE BLOOD?

TIME IN THE WORD:

Read John 13:1-20 . Write 3 interesting facts from the passage.

_____

_____

_____

What did Jesus do for his disciples?

_____

What did Jesus tell the disciples they should do in return?

_____

TIME IN SONG:

Sing [Are you Washed in the Blood (http://bit.ly/2dC5kVk)](http://bit.ly/2dC5kVk). Read the story behind it and fill out your notebook page.

TIME IN SERVICE:

Wash your mom's feet and rub lotion on them.

Wash something really dirty for your family or a neighbor.

Give your pets a bath.

©Not Consumed 2016 | When I Survey

Are You Washed in the Blood

1. Have you been to Jesus for the cleansing pow'r? Are you washed in the blood of the Lamb? Are you fully trusting in His grace this hour? Are you washed in the blood of the Lamb?
2. Are you walking daily by the Savior's side? Are you washed in the blood of the Lamb? Do you rest each moment in the Crucified? Are you washed in the blood of the Lamb?
3. When the Bridegroom cometh will your robes be white? Are you washed in the blood of the Lamb? Will your soul be ready for the mansions bright, And be washed in the blood of the Lamb?
4. Lay aside the garments that are stained with sin, And be washed in the blood of the Lamb; There's a fountain flowing for the soul unclean, O be washed in the blood of the Lamb!

Are you washed in the blood, In the...
Are you washed in the blood,

Text: Elisha A. Hoffman, 1839-1929
Tune: Elisha A. Hoffman, 1839-1929

11 9 11 9 Refrain
WASHED IN THE BLOOD
www.hymnary.org/text/have_you_been_to_jesus_for_the_cleansing

This hymn is in the public domain. You may freely use this score for personal and congregational worship. If you reproduce the score, please credit Hymnary.org as the source.

soul- cleans-ing blood of the Lamb? Are your gar-ments spot-less?
of the lamb?

Are they white as snow? Are you washed in the blood of the Lamb?

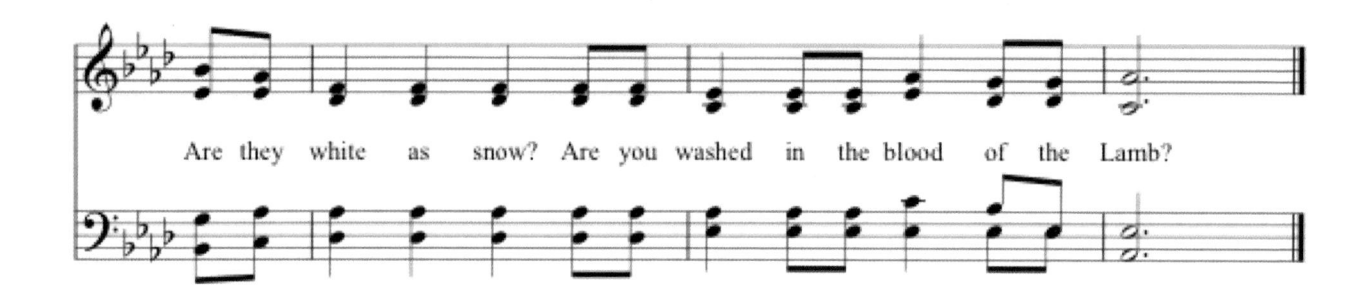

JESUS WASHED *their feet*

Use a colored pencil or crayon and trace your foot on this paper. Then ask your parent to help you find verses about feet using a concordance or online study tool. Write some of the verses you find on your foot.

DAY 2 ©Not Consumed 2016 | When I Survey

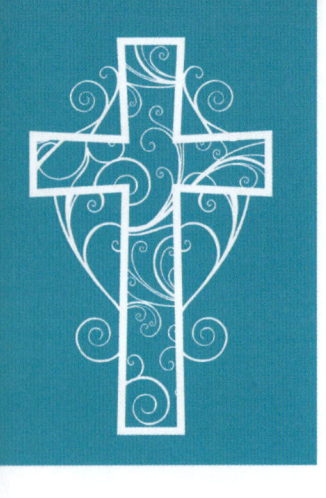

At the Cross

1 Alas! and did my Savior bleed,
and did my Sovereign die!
Would he devote that sacred head
for sinners such as I?

2 Was it for crimes that I have done,
he groaned upon the tree?
Amazing pity! Grace unknown!
And love beyond degree!

3 Well might the sun in darkness hide,
and shut its glories in,
when God, the mighty maker, died
for his own creature's sin.

4 Thus might I hide my blushing face
while his dear cross appears;
dissolve my heart in thankfulness,
and melt mine eyes to tears.

5 But drops of tears can ne'er repay
the debt of love I owe.
Here, Lord, I give myself away;
'tis all that I can do.

AT THE Cross

TIME IN THE WORD:

Read Matthew 26:17-29. Write 3 interesting facts from the passage.

_____

_____

_____

What did Jesus say the bread and wine stood for?

_____

What did Jesus tell His disciples?

_____

TIME IN SONG:

Sing At the Cross (http://bit.ly/2cXEHNj). Read the story behind it and fill out your notebook page.

TIME IN SERVICE:

Help with dinner and/or take dinner to a person who might need it. (A neighbor with a new baby, or someone who just had surgery, etc)

DAY 3 ©Not Consumed 2016 | When I Survey

THE CHURCH ON MISSION

595 At the Cross

1. A-las, and did my Sav-ior bleed, and did my Sov-ereign die?
   Would He de-vote that sa-cred head for sin-ners such as I?
2. Was it for crimes that I had done He groaned up-on the tree?
   A-maz-ing pit-y, grace un-known, and love be-yond de-gree!
3. Well might the sun in dark-ness hide, and shut his glo-ries in,
   when Christ the might-y Mak-er died for man, the crea-ture's sin.
4. Thus might I hide my blush-ing face while Cal-vary's cross ap-pears,
   dis-solve my heart in thank-ful-ness, and melt my eyes to tears.
5. But drops of grief can ne'er re-pay the debt of love I owe;
   here, Lord, I give my-self a-way, 'tis all that I can do.

Refrain:
At the cross, at the cross where I first saw the light, and the bur-den of my heart rolled a-way, rolled a-way, it was there by faith I re-ceived my sight, and now I am hap-py all the day!

WORDS: Isaac Watts, 1707; refrain Ralph E. Hudson, ca. 1885
MUSIC: John Hill Hewitt; adapt. Ralph E. Hudson, ca. 1885

HUDSON
CM with refrain

THE LAST Supper

Fill in the acrostic with words that descibes Jesus.

L _____

A _____

S _____

T _____

S _____

U _____

P _____

P _____

E _____

R _____

DAY 3 ©Not Consumed 2016 | When I Survey

In the Garden

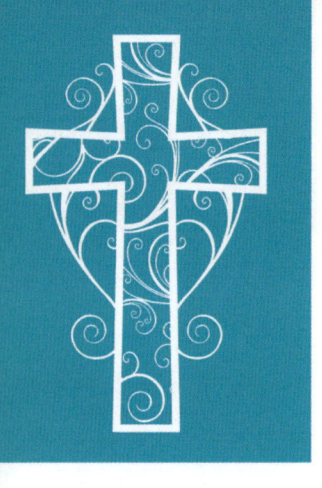

DAY 4

1 I come to the garden alone,
While the dew is still on the roses;
And the voice I hear, falling on my ear,
The Son of God discloses.

Refrain:
And He walks with me, and He talks with me,
And He tells me I am His own,
And the joy we share as we tarry there,
None other has ever known.

2 He speaks, and the sound of His voice
Is so sweet the birds hush their singing;
And the melody that He gave to me
Within my heart is ringing. [Refrain]

3 I'd stay in the garden with Him
Tho' the night around me be falling;
But He bids me go; thro' the voice of woe,
His voice to me is calling. [Refrain]

©Not Consumed 2016 | When I Survey

IN THE Garden

TIME IN THE WORD:

Read Matthew 26:36-46 . Write 3 interesting facts from the passage.

_____

_____

_____

What did Jesus ask of God (v.42)?

_____

What was Jesus frustrated about?

_____

TIME IN SONG:

Sing In the Garden (http://bit.ly/2dC9Gfq). Read the story behind it and fill out your notebook page.

TIME IN SERVICE:

Call someone and ask how you can pray for them- then do it.
Help in the garden.
Plant a flower for a friend or neighbor.

DAY 4 ©Not Consumed 2016 | When I Survey

In the GARDEN

The Bible says that, "Greater love has no one than this, that someone lay down his life for his friends." (John 15:13) Jesus' love for us was perfect. Read 1 Corinthians 13:4-8 and write the words used to describe his love around the flowers below. Draw the rest of the stems and the garden.

©Not Consumed 2016 | When I Survey

DAY 4

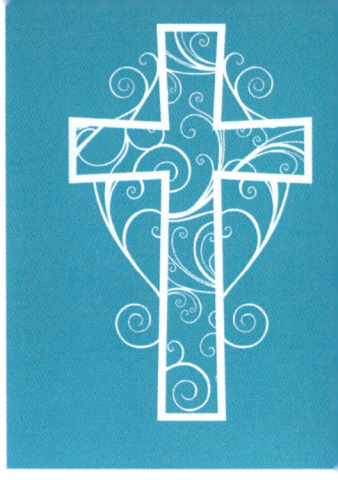

When I Survey the Wondrous Cross

DAY 5

1 When I survey the wondrous cross
on which the Prince of glory died,
my richest gain I count but loss,
and pour contempt on all my pride.

2 Forbid it, Lord, that I should boast
save in the death of Christ, my God!
All the vain things that charm me most,
I sacrifice them through his blood.

3 See, from his head, his hands, his feet,
sorrow and love flow mingled down.
Did e'er such love and sorrow meet,
or thorns compose so rich a crown?

4 Were the whole realm of nature mine,
that were a present far too small.
Love so amazing, so divine,
demands my soul, my life, my all.

©Not Consumed 2016 | When I Survey

When I Survey THE WONDROUS CROSS

TIME IN THE WORD:

Read Matthew 26:14-16, 47-50. (Optional: Read Matt. 27: 3-10) Write 3 interesting facts from the passage.

_____
_____
_____

What did Judas gain by betraying Jesus (v.15)?

_____

What did Jesus call Judas (v.50)?

_____

TIME IN SONG:

Sing When I Survey (http://bit.ly/2dE6m8U). Read the story behind it and fill out your notebook page.

TIME IN SERVICE:

Learn how to make a scratch off (http://bit.ly/2dE76ec). Send someone a scratch-off message about Jesus' love.

©Not Consumed 2016 | When I Survey

DAY 5

When I Survey the Wondrous Cross

1. When I survey the wondrous cross on which the Prince of glory died, my richest gain I count but loss, and pour contempt on all my pride.
2. Forbid it, Lord, that I should boast save in the death of Christ, my God! All the vain things that charm me most, I sacrifice them through his blood.
3. See, from his head, his hands, his feet, sorrow and love flow mingled down. Did e'er such love and sorrow meet, or thorns compose so rich a crown?
4. Were the whole realm of nature mine, that were a present far too small. Love so amazing, so divine, demands my soul, my life, my all.

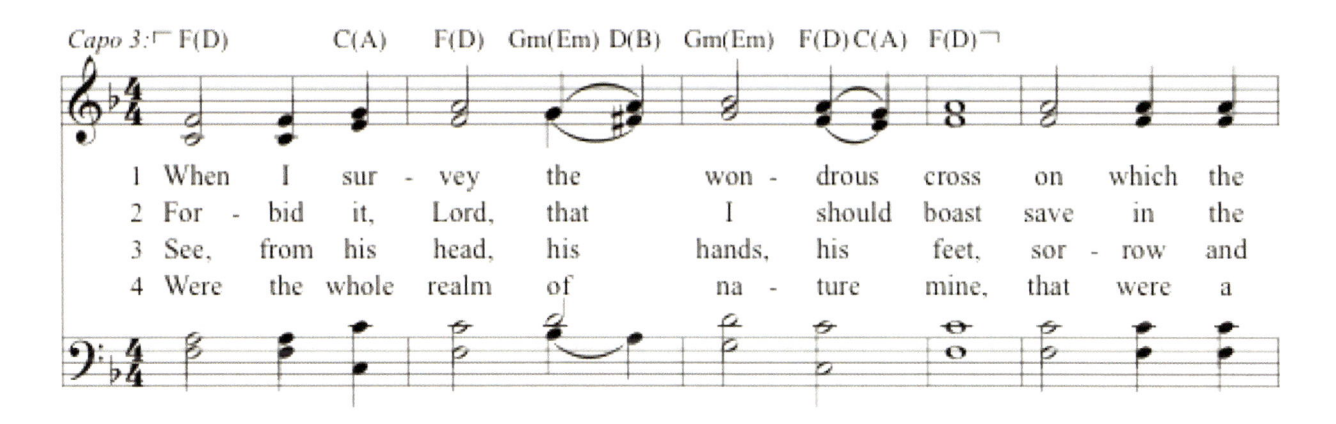

Text: Isaac Watts, 1707
Tune: Lowell Mason, 1824

LM
HAMBURG

www.hymnary.org/text/when_i_survey_the_wondrous_cross

This hymn is in the public domain. You may freely use this score for personal and congregational worship. If you reproduce the score, please credit Hymnary.org as the source.

Word Search

JUDAS BETRAYED JESUS

```
C C D N D K M W D N C N L Y J Z O F Z S
W Y V E V T O L H X Q R L K B K P D U B
S K A G U V F S N I O C C J K U I V H A
O T H V S Y H D N T Z X M W D I R M Q Q
H K V I J M Y Q C D K R Z R F C T T B X
H E R U T E V K L I D C Y J R X S O R Z
B G V R E P P U S S O H C U M S T H E D
B R Q H D G M S U C O A O S F R S J L F
P S H F L S W S P I N M I B W Q E Q M G
J Y W G M S E D V P S E E L K U I C U T
V A A O Q J P Z T L H C D I L Q R I Z H
K K D J R K G T R E P A E N W W P F Z S
C F A U M D L H C S W P H N U B B V H Y
U V A W Z A S I J H Q X E G E Y I T S R
Q A E Y R D T R X K B M P T Y B N D I J
Q C D B J T Z T W J E Q R Y D E N F G M
F D V G E M G Y H R U A T C D Y A E N L
U G V K J Z N Y Y E Y D S R O A S P Z G
H N E E P X H F G A W F A G V H W E J T
O J N Z M F L E L O W G L S M D M V Z A
```

BETRAYAL	JESUS	JUDAS
COINS	PRIESTS	THIRTY
KISS	SWORDS	MATTHEW
DISCIPLES	SIGN	DEATH
LAST	SUPPER	GARDEN

©Not Consumed 2016 | When I Survey

DAY 5

Crown Him With Many Crowns

1. Crown Him with many crowns,
The Lamb upon His throne;
Hark! How the heav'nly anthem drowns
All music but its own!
Awake, my soul and sing
Of Him Who died for thee,
And hail Him as thy matchless King
Through all eternity.

2. Crown Him the Lord of love!
Behold His hands and side—
Rich wounds, yet visible above,
In beauty glorified.
No angel in the sky
Can fully bear that sight,
But downward bends His wond'ring eye
At mysteries so bright.

3. Crown Him the Lord of life!
Who triumphed o'er the grave,
Who rose victorious in the strife
For those He came to save.
His glories now we sing,
Who died, and rose on high,
Who died eternal life to bring,
And lives that death may die.

4. Crown Him the Lord of heav'n!
One with the Father known,
One with the Spirit through Him giv'n
From yonder glorious throne,
To Thee be endless praise,
For Thou for us hast died;
Be Thou, O Lord, through endless days
Adored and magnified.

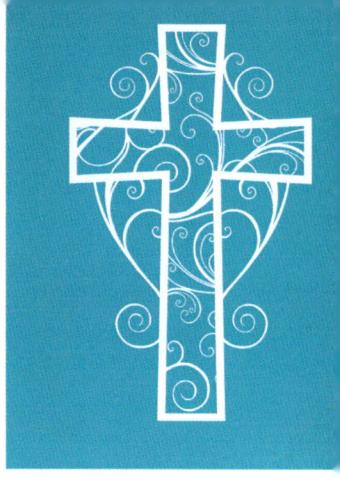

DAY 6

Crown Him WITH MANY CROWNS

TIME IN THE WORD:

Read Matt. 26:51-56, 27:27-31 (optional longer reading Matt. 26:51-68 and 27:3-31). Write 3 interesting facts from the passage.

_____
_____
_____

Why did Jesus say that all of this had taken place (v. 56)?

_____

How do you think the disciples felt in this moment?

_____

TIME IN SONG:

Sing Crown Him with Many Crowns (http://bit.ly/1fzgGn6). Read the story behind it and fill out your notebook page.

TIME IN SERVICE:

Jesus was wrongly accused. Make a card or write a note to someone that you have accused, hurt or made fun of, apologizing for your unkind behavior.

©Not Consumed 2016 | When I Survey   DAY 6

Crown Him with Many Crowns

1 Crown him with many crowns, the Lamb upon his throne.
2 Crown him the Lord of life, who triumphed o'er the grave,
3 Crown him the Lord of love; behold his hands and side,
4 Crown him the Lord of years, the potentate of time,

Hark! how the heavenly anthem drowns all music but its own.
and rose victorious in the strife for those he came to save;
rich wounds, yet visible above, in beauty glorified;
creator of the rolling spheres, ineffably sublime.

Awake, my soul, and sing of him who died for thee,
his glories now we sing who died and rose on high,
no angels in the sky can fully bear that sight,
All hail, Redeemer, hail! for thou hast died for me:

and hail him as thy matchless king through all eternity.
who died eternal life to bring, and lives that death may die.
but downward bends their burning eye at mysteries so bright.
thy praise shall never, never fail throughout eternity.

Text: Matthew Bridges (1800-1894) and
Godfrey Thring (1823-1903)
Tune: George J. Elvey (1816-1893)

SMD
DIADEMATA
www.hymnary.org/text/crown_him_with_many_crowns

This hymn is in the public domain. You may freely use this score for personal and congregational worship. If you reproduce the score, please credit *Hymnary.org* as the source.

Jesus WAS ARRESTED

Using the passage listed on your study sheet, fill in the blanks to discover the word. An ESV translation might be helpful.

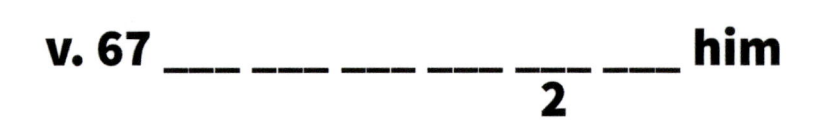

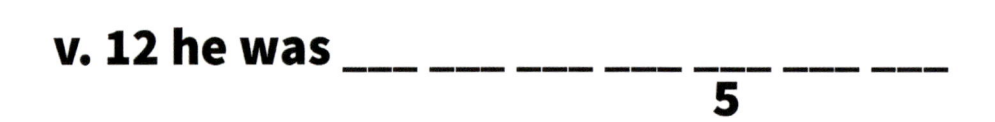

v. 67 ___ ___ ___ ___ in his face
            8

v. 67 ___ ___ ___ ___ ___ ___ him
                  2

v. 67 ___ ___ ___ ___ ___ ___ ___ him
              4

v. 12 he was ___ ___ ___ ___ ___ ___ ___
                          5

v. 29 crown of ___ ___ ___ ___ ___ ___
                        6

v. 29 ___ ___ ___ ___ ___ ___ him
                      7

v. 30 ___ ___ ___ ___ ___ ___ his head
              3

v. 31 ___ ___ ___ ___ ___ ___ ___ ___ ___ him
                      9   1

Jesus was the ___ ___ ___ ___ ___ ___ ___ ___ ___.
              5   4   3   6   9   1   8   2   7

©Not Consumed 2016 | When I Survey

DAY 6

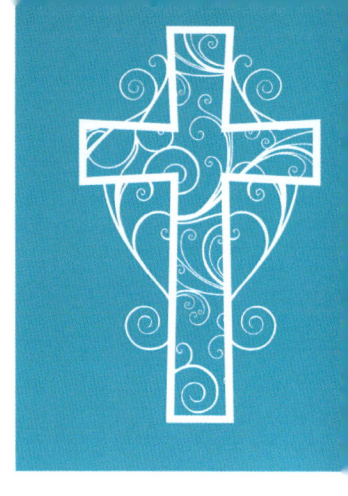

Grace Greater Than Our Sin

DAY 7

1 Marvelous grace of our loving Lord,
grace that exceeds our sin and our guilt,
yonder on Calvary's mount out-poured,
there where the blood of the Lamb was spilt.

Refrain:
Grace, grace, God's grace,
grace that will pardon and cleanse within;
grace, grace, God's grace,
grace that is greater than all our sin.

2 Dark is the stain that we cannot hide,
what can avail to wash it away!
Look! there is flowing a crimson tide;
whiter than snow you may be today. [Refrain]

3 Marvelous, infinite, matchless grace,
freely bestowed on all who believe;
you that are longing to see his face,
will you this moment his grace receive? [Refrain]

Grace GREATER THAN OUR SINS

TIME IN THE WORD:

Read Matt. 26:69-75. Write 3 interesting facts from the passage.

_____
_____
_____

What did Peter do when he was asked if he was with Jesus?

_____

What did Peter do once he realized his sin (v.75)?

_____

TIME IN SONG:

Sing Grace Greater Than Our Sin (http://bit.ly/2dLkjkR). Read the story behind it and fill out your notebook page.

TIME IN SERVICE:

Pray for and write an encouraging letter to a missionary in a dangerous area standing up for Jesus.

©Not Consumed 2016 | When I Survey   DAY 7

Grace Greater than Our Sin

1. Mar-ve-lous grace of our lo-ving Lord,
grace that ex-ceeds our sin and our guilt!
Yon-der on Cal-va-ry's mount out-poured,
there where the blood of the Lamb was spilt.

2. Sin and des-pair, like the sea waves cold,
threa-ten the soul with in-fi-nite loss;
grace that is grea-ter, yes, grace un-told,
points to the re-fuge, the migh-ty cross.

3. Dark is the stain that we can-not hide.
What can a-vail to wash it a-way?
Look! There is flo-wing a crim-son tide,
brigh-ter than snow you may be to-day.

4. Mar-ve-lous, in-fi-nite, match-less grace,
free-ly bes-towed on all who be-lieve!
You that are long-ing to see his face,
will you this mo-ment his grace re-ceive?

Text: Julia H. Johnston, 1911
Tune: Daniel B. Towner, 1910

99 99 Refrain
MOODY

www.hymnary.org/text/marvelous_grace_of_our_loving_lord

This hymn is in the public domain. You may freely use this score for personal and congregational worship. If you reproduce the score, please credit Hymnary.org as the source.

Refrain
Grace, grace, God's grace, grace that will par - don and
cleanse with - in; grace, grace, God's grace,
grace that is grea - ter than all our sin!

PETER DENIES Jesus

Unscramble the words below. Use Matthew 26:69-75 (ESV) to help you.

1. **ujsse of arthnzae** _____

2. **ejuss** _____

3. **rsantve rgil** _____

4. **crtodayur** _____

5. **trpee** _____

6. **osrteor swcor** _____

7. **enided** _____

8. **hreet** _____

9. **wresa** _____

10. **eptw** _____

DAY 3 ©Not Consumed 2016 | When I Survey

There is a Fountain

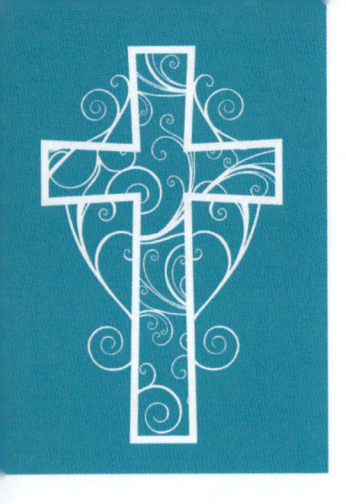

DAY 8

1 1 There is a fountain filled with blood
Drawn from Immanuel's veins;
And sinners, plunged beneath that flood,
Lose all their guilty stains:
Lose all their guilty stains,
Lose all their guilty stains;
And sinners, plunged beneath that flood,
Lose all their guilty stains.

2 The dying thief rejoiced to see
That fountain in his day;
And there may I, though vile as he,
Wash all my sins away:
Wash all my sins away,
Wash all my sins away;
And there may I, though vile as he,
Wash all my sins away.

3 Dear dying Lamb, Thy precious blood
Shall never lose its pow'r,
Till all the ransomed Church of God
Be saved, to sin no more:
Be saved, to sin no more,
Be saved, to sin no more;
Till all the ransomed Church of God
Be saved to sin no more.

4 E'er since by faith I saw the stream
Thy flowing wounds supply,
Redeeming love has been my theme,
And shall be till I die:
And shall be till I die,
And shall be till I die;
Redeeming love has been my theme,
And shall be till I die.

5 When this poor lisping, stamm'ring tongue
Lies silent in the grave,
Then in a nobler, sweeter song
I'll sing Thy pow'r to save:
I'll sing Thy pow'r to save,
I'll sing Thy pow'r to save;
then in a nobler, sweeter song
I'll sing Thy pow'r to save.

THERE IS A Fountain

TIME IN THE WORD:

Read Luke 23:32-43. Write 3 interesting facts from the passage.

_____

_____

_____

What was the attitude of the 1st criminal who spoke?

_____

What was the attitude of the 2nd?

_____

TIME IN SONG:

Sing There is a Fountain (http://bit.ly/1OdYrZn). Read the story behind it and fill out your notebook page.

TIME IN SERVICE:

Learn (or practice) the Romans road so you will be ready to give an answer to anyone with questions about God. Then pass out a tract to someone who doesn't know Jesus and/or tell them about what HE has done for you!

DAY 8

There Is a Fountain Filled with Blood

1. There is a foun-tain filled with blood Drawn from Im-ma-nuel's veins;
2. The dy-ing thief re-joiced to see That foun-tain in his day;
3. Dear dy-ing Lamb, Thy pre-cious blood Shall ne-ver lose its pow'r,
4. E'er since by faith I saw the stream Thy flo-wing wounds sup-ply,
5. When this poor lis-ping, stamm'-ring tongue Lies si-lent in the grave,

And sin-ners, plunged be-neath that flood, Lose all their guil-ty stains:
And there may I, though vile as he, Wash all my sins a-way:
Till all the ran-somed Church of God Be saved, to sin no more.
Re-deem-ing love has been my theme, And shall be till I die:
Then in a no-bler, swee-ter song I'll sing Thy pow'r to save:

Lose all their guil-ty stains, Lose all their guil-ty stains; And
Wash all my sins a-way, Wash all my sins a-way; And
Be saved, to sin no more, Be saved, to sin no more; Till
And shall be till I die, And shall be till I die; Re
I'll sing Thy pow'r to save, I'll sing Thy pow'r to save; then

sin-ners, plunged be-neath that flood, Lose all their guil-ty stains.
there may I, though vile as he, Wash all my sins a-way.
all the ran-somed Church of God Be saved to sin no more.
deem-ing love has been my theme, And shall be till I die.
in a no-bler, swee-ter song I'll sing Thy pow'r to save. A-men.

Text: William Cowper (1731-1800)
Tune: Traditional american melody;
arr. Lowell Mason (1792-1872)

86 86 66 86
CLEANSING FOUNTAIN
www.hymnary.org/there_is_a_fountain_filled_with_blood_dr

This hymn is in the public domain. You may freely use this score for personal and congregational worship. If you reproduce the score, please credit Hymnary.org as the source.

ROMANS ROAD TO Salvation

Use the Bible to fill in the blanks. Then practice the verses so you can share the good news with someone who is lost.

Romans 3:10
As it is written, there is none righteous, no _____ _____.

Romans 3:23
For _____ have sinned and fall short of the glory of God.

Romans 5:12
Therefore, just as sin came into the world through _____ _____, and death through sin, and so death spread to all men because all sinned—

Romans 6:23
For the wages of sin is _____, but the free gift of God is eternal life in Christ Jesus our Lord.

Romans 5:8
but God shows his love for us in that while we were still sinners, _____ died for us.

Romans 10:9-10
[9] because, if you confess with your mouth that Jesus is Lord and believe in your heart that God raised him from the dead, you will be _____. [10] For with the heart one believes and is justified, and with the mouth one confesses and is saved.

Romans 10:13
For "_____ who calls on the name of the Lord will be saved."

DAY 8 ©Not Consumed 2016 | When I Survey

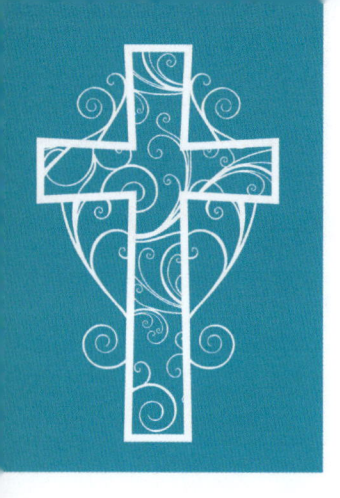

DAY 9

Jesus Paid It All

1 I hear the Savior say,
"Thy strength indeed is small,
Child of weakness, watch and pray,
Find in Me thine all in all."

Refrain:
Jesus paid it all,
All to Him I owe;
Sin had left a crimson stain,
He washed it white as snow.

2 Lord, now indeed I find
Thy pow'r and Thine alone,
Can change the leper's spots
And melt the heart of stone. [Refrain]

3 For nothing good have I
Where-by Thy grace to claim;
I'll wash my garments white
In the blood of Calv'ry's Lamb. [Refrain]

4 And when, before the throne,
I stand in Him complete,
"Jesus died my soul to save,"
My lips shall still repeat. [Refrain]

©Not Consumed 2016 | When I Survey

JESUS Paid It All

TIME IN THE WORD:

Read Matthew 27:45-56. Write 3 interesting facts from the passage.

_____

_____

_____

Did Jesus die unwillingly (v. 50)?

_____

What did the centurion say about Jesus once He died (v.54)?

_____

TIME IN SONG:

Sing [Jesus Paid It All (http://bit.ly/2d90RtJ).](http://bit.ly/2d90RtJ) Read the story behind it and fill out your notebook page.

TIME IN SERVICE:

Jesus suffered an awful death so that we would be blessed with forgiveness of our sins. Today, do something you hate doing so that someone else will be blessed. (Maybe clean the toilets, wash dishes, clean out the trash cans.) Don't forget to do it with a happy heart!

Jesus Paid It All

1. I hear the Savior say, "Thy stength indeed is small,
Child of weakness, watch and pray, Find in Me thine all in all."

2. Lord, now indeed I find Thy pow'r and Thine alone,
Can change the leper's spots And melt the heart of stone.

3. For nothing good have I Whereby Thy grace to claim;
I'll wash my garments white In the blood of Cal-v'ry's Lamb.

4. And when, before the throne, I stand in Him complete,
"Jesus died my soul to save," My lips shall still repeat.

Refrain
Jesus paid it all, All to Him I owe;
Sin had left a crimson stain, He washed it white as snow.

Text: Elvina M. Hall, 1820-1889
Tune: John T. Grape, 1835-1915

Irregular
ALL TO CHRIST

This hymn is in the public domain. You may freely use this score for personal and congregational worship. If you reproduce the score, please credit Hymnary.org as the source.

JESUS DIED FOR *my sins*

Write some of your sins on the cross. As you write, thank God for forgiving you for that sin.

DAY 9

Low in the Grave He Lay

1 Low in the grave he lay, Jesus my Savior,
waiting the coming day, Jesus my Lord!

Refrain:
Up from the grave he arose;
with a mighty triumph o'er his foes;
he arose a victor from the dark domain,
and he lives forever, with his saints to reign.
He arose! He arose! Hallelujah! Christ arose!

2 Vainly they watch his bed, Jesus my Savior,
vainly they seal the dead, Jesus my Lord!
[Refrain]

3 Death cannot keep its prey, Jesus my Savior;
he tore the bars away, Jesus my Lord! [Refrain]

LOW IN THE GROUND He lay

TIME IN THE WORD:

Read Matt. 27: 57-66. Write 3 interesting facts from the passage.

_____

_____

_____

What did Joseph of Arimathea do for Jesus?

_____

What did the Pharisees insist that Pilate do and why?

_____

TIME IN SONG:

Sing Low in the Grave He Lay (http://bit.ly/2dLqqWs). Read the story behind it and fill out your notebook page.

TIME IN SERVICE:

Joseph of Arimathea gave up something very important to his family so that Jesus would have a proper tomb. Give up something important today so that someone else will have something special.

DAY 10 ©Not Consumed 2016 | When I Survey

Low in the Grave Christ Lay

1. Low in the grave Christ lay— Jesus, my Savior;
waiting the coming day—
2. Vainly they watch his bed— Jesus, my Savior;
vainly they seal the dead— Jesus, my Lord.
3. Death cannot keep its prey— Jesus, my Savior;
he tore the bars away—

Refrain:
Up from the grave he a-rose, with a mighty triumph o'er his foes;
he a-rose!

Text and tune by Robert Lowry, 1874, alt.

65 64 with refrain
CHRIST AROSE
www.hymnary.org/text/low_in_the_grave_he_lay_jesus_my_savior

This hymn is in the public domain. You may freely use this score for personal and congregational worship. If you reproduce the score, please credit Hymnary.org as the source.

Page 2 — Low in the Grave Christ Lay

(Sheet music)

Lyrics:
foes, He arose a victor from the dark domain, he arose! and he lives forever with his saints to reign! He arose! He arose! He arose! Hallelujah! Christ arose! He arose!

Jesus IN THE GRAVE

Can you imagine how everyone must have felt when they buried Jesus in the tomb? Use colored strips of construction paper and write words to describe how the different people must have felt. For example: Mary, Peter, Pilate, Judas, the Centurion, Pharisees, etc. Glue the strips to the tomb.

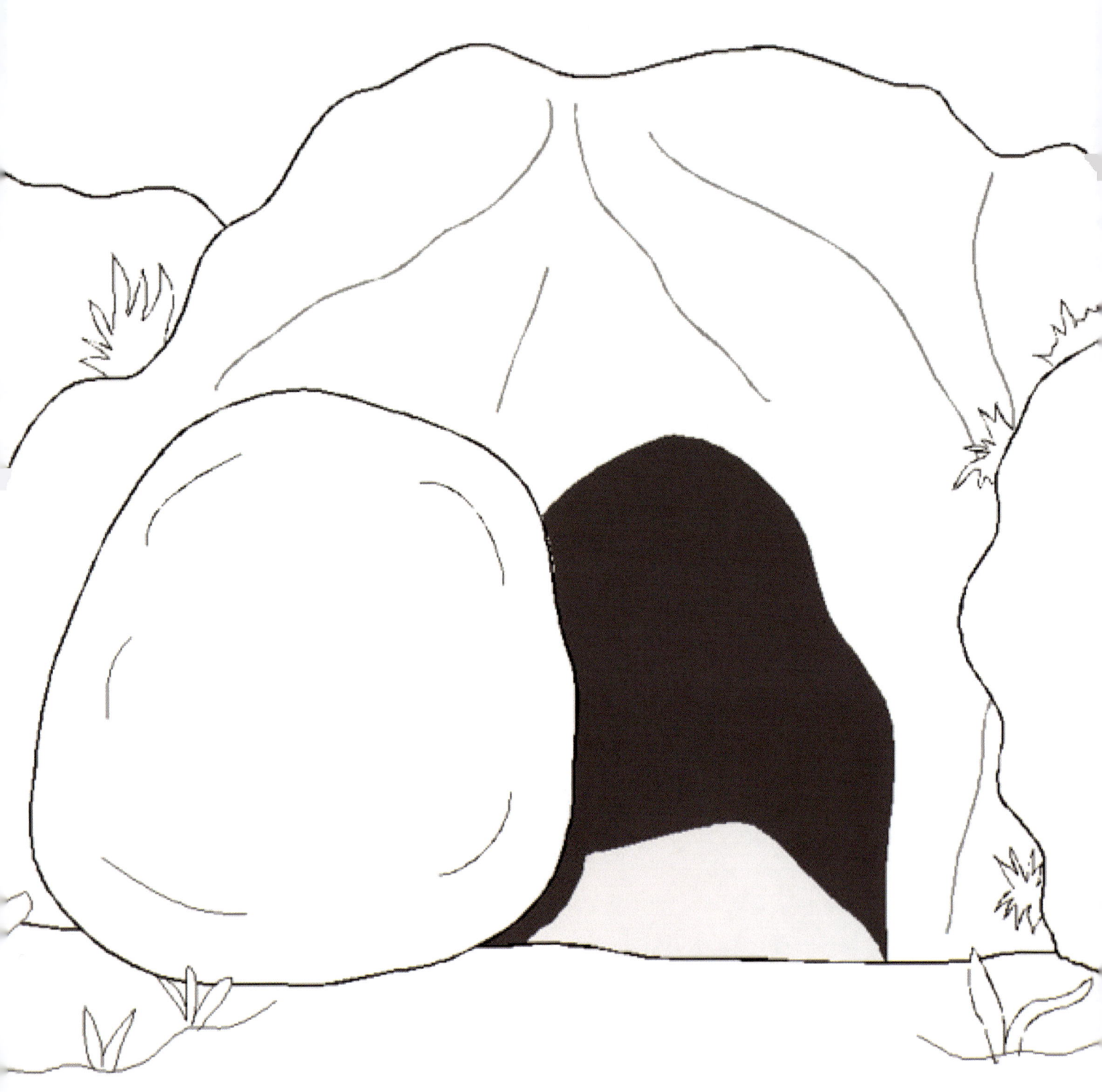

Christ the Lord is Risen Today

1 Christ the Lord is risen today, Alleluia!
Earth and heaven in chorus say, Alleluia!
Raise your joys and triumphs high, Alleluia!
Sing, ye heavens, and earth reply, Alleluia!

2 Love's redeeming work is done, Alleluia!
Fought the fight, the battle won, Alleluia!
Death in vain forbids him rise, Alleluia!
Christ has opened paradise, Alleluia!

3 Lives again our glorious King, Alleluia!
Where, O death, is now thy sting? Alleluia!
Once he died our souls to save, Alleluia!
Where's thy victory, boasting grave? Alleluia!

4 Soar we now where Christ has led, Alleluia!
Following our exalted Head, Alleluia!
Made like him, like him we rise, Alleluia!
Ours the cross, the grave, the skies, Alleluia!

5 Hail the Lord of earth and heaven, Alleluia!
Praise to thee by both be given, Alleluia!
Thee we greet triumphant now, Alleluia!
Hail the Resurrection, thou, Alleluia!

6 King of glory, soul of bliss, Alleluia!
Everlasting life is this, Alleluia!
Thee to know, thy power to prove, Alleluia!
Thus to sing, and thus to love, Alleluia!

DAY 11

©Not Consumed 2016 | When I Survey

Christ the Lord IS RISEN TODAY

TIME IN THE WORD:

Read Matthew 28:1-20. Write 3 interesting facts from the passage.

_____

_____

_____

What did the angel say to Mary?

_____

How did the priest try to cover the truth (v.13)?

_____

TIME IN SONG:

Sing Christ the Lord is Risen Today (http://bit.ly/2dUSy8N). Read the story behind it and fill out your notebook page.

TIME IN SERVICE:

Mary and Mary Magdalene were coming to visit the grave of Jesus when they got the news. It can be very lonely when a loved one dies. Do you know a widow? Find out from your church about someone that you might visit. Take her a card or a special treat and spend time with her.

Christ the Lord Is Risen Today

1. Christ the Lord is ris'n to-day, Alleluia!
Sons of men and an-gels say, Alleluia!
Raise your joys and tri-umphs high, Alleluia!
Sing, ye heav'ns, and earth, re-ply, Alleluia!

2. Lives a-gain our glo-rious King, Alleluia!
Where, O Death, is now thy sting? Alleluia!
Dy-ing once he all doth save, Alleluia!
Where thy vic-to-ry, O Grave? Alleluia!

3. Love's re-deem-ing work is done, Alleluia!
Fought the fight, the bat-tle won, Alleluia!
Death in vain for-bids Him rise, Alleluia!
Christ hath o-pened pa-ra-dise, Alleluia!

4. Soar we now where Christ has led, Alleluia!
Foll'-wing our ex-al-ted Head, Alleluia!
Made like Him, like Him we rise, Alleluia!
Ours the cross, the grave, the skies, Alleluia!

Text: Charles Wesley, 1707-1788
Tune: *Lyra Davidica*, 1708

77 77 Alleluias
EASTER HYMN
www.hymnary.org/text/christ_the_lord_is_risen_today_wesley

This hymn is in the public domain. You may freely use this score for personal and congregational worship. If you reproduce the score, please credit *hymnary.org* as the source.

Christ's RESURRECTION

How many different words can you make from the letters in the phrase "Christ's Resurrection"? Write them on the lines below. Hint: you can write the letters on paper and cut them out to make titles. Them move them around to make new words.

He Lives

DAY 12

1 I serve a risen Savior,
he's in the world today;
I know that he is living,
whatever others say;
I see his hand of mercy,
I hear his voice of cheer,
and just the time I need him
he's always near.

Refrain:
He lives, he lives,
Christ Jesus lives today!
He walks with me and talks with me
along life's narrow way.
He lives, he lives, salvation to impart!
You ask me how I know he lives?
He lives within my heart.

2 In all the world around me
I see his loving care,
and though my heart grows weary,
I never will despair;
I know that he is leading
through all the stormy blast,
the day of his appearing
will come at last. [Refrain]

3 Rejoice, rejoice, O Christian,
lift up your voice and sing
eternal hallelujahs
to Jesus Christ the King!
The hope of all who seek him,
the help of all who find,
no other is so loving,
so good and kind. [Refrain]

©Not Consumed 2016　|　When I Survey

He LIVES

TIME IN THE WORD:

Read Revelation 1:7-8. Write 3 interesting facts from the passage.

_____

_____

_____

What do you think is the most exciting thing about Jesus being alive?

_____

What does Revelation say that we have to look forward to?

_____

TIME IN SONG:

Sing He Lives (http://bit.ly/2cNV2kp) Read the story behind it and fill out your notebook page.

TIME IN SERVICE:

The time of Jesus' return is unknown. Write an encouraging note to someone in your family and hide it in their Bible. Just like Jesus' return, you will never know just when they might find it!

©Not Consumed 2016 | When I Survey

DAY 12

285 He Lives

...That I may know Him, and the power of His resurrection. Phil. 3:10

ALFRED H. ACKLEY   ALFRED H. ACKLEY

1. I serve a risen Savior, He's in the world today; I know that He is living, whatever men may say; I see His hand of mercy, I hear His voice of cheer, And just the time I need Him He's always near.

2. In all the world around me I see His loving care, And tho' my heart grows weary, I never will despair; I know that He is leading thro' all the stormy blast, The day of His appearing will come at last.

3. Rejoice, rejoice, O Christian, lift up your voice and sing Eternal hallelujahs to Jesus Christ the King! The Hope of all who seek Him, the Help of all who find, None other is so loving, so good and kind.

Refrain

He lives, He lives, Christ Jesus lives today! He walks with me and talks with me along life's narrow way. He lives, He lives, sal-
He lives, He lives,   He lives, He lives,

© Copyright 1933 by Homer A. Rodeheaver. © Renewed 1961 by The Rodeheaver Co. (A Div. of WORD, INC.) All Rights Reserved. International Copyright Secured. Used by Permission.

Jesus WILL RETURN

The Bible says that Jesus will come back someday with the clouds (Rev 1:7-8). When you think about that day, what are you looking forward to? Write it on the clouds.

DAY 12

APPENDIX

COPYWORK IN KJV Print

Copywork KJV

...Blessed is he that cometh in the name of the Lord; Hosanna in the highest. Matthew 21:9

Verily, verily, I say unto you, The servant is not greater than his lord; neither he that is sent greater than he that sent him. John 13:16

Copywork KJV

For this is my blood of the new testament, which is shed for many for the remission of sins. Matthew 26:28

Copywork KJV

Watch and pray, that ye enter not into temptation: the spirit indeed is willing, but the flesh is weak. Matthew 26:41

Copywork KJV

But all this was done, that the scriptures of the prophets might be fulfilled. Then all the disciples forsook him, and fled. Matthew 26:56

Copywork KJV

Jesus saith unto him, Thou hast said: nevertheless I say unto you, Hereafter shall ye see the Son of man sitting on the right hand of power, and coming in the clouds of heaven. Matthew 26:64

Copywork KJV

Moreover the law entered, that the offence might abound. But where sin abounded, grace did much more abound: Romans 5:20

Copywork KJV

That if thou shalt confess with thy mouth the Lord Jesus, and shalt believe in thine heart that God hath raised him from the dead, thou shalt be saved. Romans 10:9

Copywork KJV

And, behold, the veil of the temple was rent in twain from the top to the bottom; and the earth did quake, and the rocks rent; Matthew 27:51

Then took they the body of Jesus, and wound it in linen clothes with the spices, as the manner of the Jews is to bury.
John 19:40

Copywork — KJV

He is not here: for he is risen, as he said. Come, see the place where the Lord lay.
Matthew 28:6

Copywork | KJV

Behold, he cometh with clouds; and every eye shall see him, and they also which pierced him: and all kindreds of the earth shall wail because of him. Even so, Amen. Revelation 1:7

APPENDIX

COPYWORK IN ESV Print

Copywork ESV

"Hosanna to the Son of David! Blessed is he who comes in the name of the Lord! Hosanna in the highest!" Matthew 21:9

Copywork ESV

Truly, truly, I say to you, a servant is not greater than his master, nor is a messenger greater than the one who sent him. John 13:16

Copywork ESV

for this is my blood of the covenant, which is poured out for many for the forgiveness of sins. Matthew 26:28

Copywork ESV

Watch and pray that you may not enter into temptation. The spirit indeed is willing, but the flesh is weak." Matthew 26:41

Copywork ESV

But all this has taken place that the Scriptures of the prophets might be fulfilled." Then all the disciples left him and fled.
Matthew 26:56

Copywork ESV

Jesus said to him, "You have said so. But I tell you, from now on you will see the Son of Man seated at the right hand of Power and coming on the clouds of heaven." Matthew 26:64

Copywork ESV

Now the law came in to increase the trespass, but where sin increased, grace abounded all the more, Romans 5:20

Copywork ESV

because, if you confess with your mouth that Jesus is Lord and believe in your heart that God raised him from the dead, you will be saved. Romans 10:9

Copywork — ESV

And behold, the curtain of the temple was torn in two, from top to bottom. And the earth shook, and the rocks were split. Matthew 27:51

Copywork ESV

So they took the body of Jesus and bound it in linen cloths with the spices, as is the burial custom of the Jews. John 19:40

Copywork ESV

He is not here, for he has risen, as he said. Come, see the place where he lay.
Matthew 28:6

Copywork ESV

Behold, he is coming with the clouds, and every eye will see him, even those who pierced him, and all tribes of the earth will wail on account of him. Even so. Amen. Revelation 1:7

Made in the USA
Charleston, SC
12 October 2016